THE UNION OF
GEOMETRY & ASH

Jill—

Thanks for the friendship
& support.

Best,

Joel B____

THE UNION OF GEOMETRY & ASH

JOSH BOOTON

THE DOROTHY BRUNSMAN POETRY PRIZE
BEAR STAR PRESS
COHASSET, CALIFORNIA

THE UNION OF GEOMETRY & ASH © 2013 BY JOSH BOOTON

Printed on archival paper in the United States of America.

10 9 8 7 6 5 4 3 2 1

Inquiries can be directed to the publisher:
BEAR STAR PRESS
185 Hollow Oak Drive
Cohasset, CA 95973
530.891.0360 / www.bearstarpress.com

Cover photograph from iStockphoto
Cover design: Josh Booton & Beth Spencer
Book design: Beth Spencer
Author photograph: K. Schultz

The book is set in Gill Sans & Minion Pro.
Printing by BookMobile in Minneapolis, MN.

Bear Star books are available from the press (www.bearstarpress.com)
and Small Press Distribution (www.spdbooks.org).

ISBN: 978-0-9850584-4-9
Library of Congress Control Number: 2013933782

The publisher would like to thank Dorothy Brunsman
for her support of the press from its inception.

For Kristin

CONTENTS

Longing is the agony of the nearness of the distant.

—Heidegger

LOVE EQUATIONS

If each loss is feathered into the next, then

> the blind girl with grand mal seizures
> is second cousin to the sea.

If all our secret speeches were leaked
to the evening news, then

> we wouldn't navigate these days
> by icebergs only.

If silence is always tinctured with a touch
of crowsong, then

> a stop sign in the middle of nowhere.

If my name were the name the Korean woman yells
to call her Labrador home at dusk, then

> the simple zodiac of streetlights
> would govern me through this life.

If each shadow is an entity
all its own, then

> we are only green's urge to elm.

If the man with SWEETPEE tattooed on his bicep
had consulted a dictionary, then

> love would be a subdivision
> just off the freeway.

If the ocean relinquishes one inch each year,
then

a man wakes to the sound of a woman, his wife,
singing in the other room, some blues
or hymnal, a pop song from his childhood,

then

he throws back the rose-embroidered blanket
as if undoing his own death, and inches
toward the door. He stops. Just short of where
the words might come clear. Knowing

if he draws any closer, then

her singing will step into a song.

one

A PIECE OF PAPER ON THE INTERSTATE

Something wounded in the way
it flutters and dives, revealing
the wake of 18-wheelers
with one wide arc
that reminds me of
a deaf girl's hands, the sign
for evening, which is almost
here, the traffic slowing
so we can taper ourselves
into the tunnel
that leads toward night.
Or the way the paper turns
now, alternating
front to back, the sign
for tree, as leaves
in wind, a single sheet
dreaming itself
back into the forest.
It's probably nothing
but a grocery list, a phone number
no longer needed, though
I hope a little
it's a love letter addressed
to the inmate crew
who will clean the roadside
later this week, an SOS
from the young widow
seven cars ahead.
I'd go to her now,
wade with her through
this momentary ocean
of cars, carry her
as we both are

carried toward whatever
shore will take us, the tiny
island of her bed,
where I tuck her snugly
beneath a paper-white sheet.
Or maybe we just hold
each other, practicing
the mild origami
that intimacy is, overlapping
ourselves until
her despair means my keys
on the side table, my longing,
the arches of her feet.
Until her soft sobs turn
to car horns and traffic
picks up again, and I remember
she doesn't exist. Only
this piece of paper
that touches a moment
the ground, then is gone.

FINCHES

Because my father kept thirty-seven finches
in a man-sized cage
in my childhood home, I dream
most nights of flight, the city black below
except a few houselights like some ragged zodiac
I almost recognize before I fall back
into that snug room on Steel Street.
Because my father left West Virginia
the year the strip miners tore the last hill down,
he harbors the dark of mine shafts in his eyes
and teaches me the names
for flowers and stars. What were we driving to find
those mornings through
the puddle-dark streets of Southeast Portland, past
empty parks and used car lots,
past the bums stuttering up Sandy with their stolen
grocery carts and heaps of gleaming cans?
He'd go in alone, fetch some channel locks or insecticide
and a bag of gizzards we'd pass between us
like tokens, bullion fished from the ribcage
of sunken colonial clipper ships,
our inner-most secrets. *Bullshit,*
I can hear him say, shifting into fifth,
eat it before it gets cold.
Is my manhood really contingent
upon his death? Was it enough
that I borrowed his flannels without asking
and eloped into grunge, heisted his pipe
and puffed hibiscus? Will any death do? Probably not
the psychic kind but some violence
ornery enough that only a swagger will keep it
at arm's length. Even that afternoon
I stood beside his hospital bed watching the nurse

as she peeled back the bandage, the single wing
that concealed an eight-inch wound
where they went in
with their crowbars and their welding torch
and scraped clean those coal-dark corridors
until his heart walls glowed
like Chinese lanterns
drifting down some river with an impossible name
on a day when two virgins marry or the dead
come back dressed as peach trees.
Forgive me.
This type of reverie is a town found only by detour,
the Sunset tunnel closed that morning
we barreled down the back streets that hedge the zoo
and out of nowhere
the rose gardens flared
like all those minor fires we survive each other for.
Dad: It's December here in Texas and strangely cold.
The stars loom huge, one of those nights
when God cranks up the wattage,
as you would say, to take a better look.
Like that time the manager cut back the boxwoods
that fronted our rental, and winter showed up,
the windows chattering like teeth.
Within a day the finches were dead.
That night I didn't dream but stayed awake
listening to those sudden muffled notes,
that impossible pulse doled out over many hours
as each bird froze on its perch, then fell.
Who knows what it means? Not me.
In the morning, in socked feet, I crept out
and peered down through the bars. But the cage was clean.

THE BOOK OF LOVE

It's all wrong, the climax arriving at the close of the first chapter
and after that the lovers
always saying, *remember when.* Then
two hundred pages describing the precise arrangement
of wildflowers in a coke can on the old oak table,
how, if you lean in close and huff
the half-dead blooms, their perfume is both
clover honey and the dark
earth from which they were plucked.
Sure, the minor characters all sparkle and spit, but
read a second time, it's clear
they were lifted from Dickens, their peccadilloes only
parade floats our lovers wave and throw candy from.
Now comes the chapter of quarrels, chapter three.
Don't worry, in chapter five
they'll drink cappuccino in a quaint patisserie
and he'll cover his face and weep into his cupped hands,
and after, she'll sip his tears
and be restored. Chapter four? It contains a single word:
longing. The last chapter repeats this theme.
The rest is a thousand hand-scrawled pages
of prologue and notes. For example, on page 316,
when she hangs their sheets out to dry and the wind
tears them to the ground,
the reference states, in the Victorian tradition
this is a harbinger of death
or the first day of fall. It's only a book. Maybe
they leave the sheets in the grass
and invite the neighbors for a picnic.
Maybe they go back inside and make love or beef stroganoff.
To tell the truth, I've never
read the whole thing through. But I
remember this scene where he offers her his sweater,

even though he's naked underneath
and a little sick, and she unravels it until
there's only a single yellow thread and ties it
around both their wrists. Or was that the night we met? Was it
a sugar packet you offered me
or your heart? All I remember are those
green eyes, your imitation of a camel,
that bus-line bungalow stuffed with books. And then you
lean in close and whisper, *it wasn't like that at all.*
The house was on Hart Street,
the yellow sweater was a bus ticket. And so
we talk all night about rhapsody and trees.
And each word between us means
less than we mean it to. Therefore, we understand each other perfectly.

TAKE THIS WALTZ

Tonight, I could love you like hipsters love Pabst.
You, in the corner booth, with that full beard
I've always wanted, those second-hand rags
that never fit me right. Tonight, I could take you
home and read you poems more sophisticated
than this one, poems where love is
the other subject and so you feel it even more
like a woman you can't have, and so must.
But I'd rather we just shove
all these tables back and hold each other close.
Make those couples move. It's OK. There's no way
for two straight men to parade their affections
without a few people getting out of their seats.
Just hold me close. Let's dance like middle school,
turning slowly around, around in such tiny circles.
Isn't that what lovers do? Isn't this
the part where we raise our clutched hands
to make a doorway and you spin me twice
beneath the lintel? Once to enter a pact, once more
to enter a world where there's no need
for pacts. Close your eyes and pretend
those clinking glasses sing our secret chandelier.
You can't? It's OK. Hold me closer. Tight as you can.
As if we weren't strangers. As if we weren't men.

STRANGE SHAPES THE NIGHT MAKES

You might as well call it my surrogate heart, this hydraulic press
stamping plastic molds and time, the graveyard crew
so used to it
they bullshit non-stop over the pumps,
slipping a quick hand in
to fetch the forms and check and trim the excess
with a paring knife
as the hopper drops another inch
and the foreman, circulating, drops his safety glasses
lower on his nose, and eyes me,
eyes the stack
I'm supposed to keep
from backing up in the chute
but can't, as the woman beside me laughs in Spanish
and runs a bent finger over the cut
to check the edge is true.
It's crazy, these people toiling all night like the lesser dreams
of the sleeping millions,
shaving dowels and end caps, snapping
the excess from a sheet of model airplane parts
as if this tedium were somehow essential
to a little boy's conception of flight,
as if the foreman outshouting the generator
might span the decades
between me and *las mujeres*,
might rig my slow hands with some facility.
But I only partly catch what he says because the plates
crash down again,
because I'm seventeen, saving for that bungee-cord Ford
and a rearview vision
of the factory receding into myth, those faces
grown more faint than streetlights at noon.
The summer will be over soon.
Soon someone will take my place

at station eight, someone
with hands like hers and news from Guadalajara.
A last drag of light loiters in the parking lot
as the machines start up,
as the gossip starts up in the same spot they left it
last night, next to the knives and safety glasses, and her hands
parse what is needed
from what is not: her right hand mercy, her left hand
grief, my right hand shifting into fifth,
my left reaching
to roll the window down to feel time against my face,
to decipher the wind which is
nothing like her voice but reminds me somehow of her teasing—
pobrecito, pobrecito—
as I run my finger over the lip of the knob, the plastic
so smooth you'd never guess where
the excess was shaved,
so perfect you'd never know she existed.

MY UNCLE'S HANDS, MY FATHER'S THOUGHTS

If my voice is a whisper
   beneath the rev

of a chainsaw, my uncle
   is teaching me the names

of trees. And which burn
   hottest, their heartwood

dense as a bicep,
   the cables of his forearm

as he sets his Stihl down
   on a fresh-cut stump,

ashes his cigarette
   into the dent a fallen snag

stamped into his hard hat.
   He motions for me

to come close, to wander
   among the men

as if my tiny hands
   could set a choker,

to traverse the slash piles
   and miles of logging roads

from here to Estacada,
   from my world to his.

§

In the field guide
    my father studies, the trees

are black and white,
    the families delineated

by the texture of bark,
    by flower or fruit

or the region where they thrive.
    Each from the other

by the county lines
    of a hand-drawn leaf.

§

If I am nine in this memory,
     my uncle is rooting

through his workshop, hunting
     for my birthday present.

My father gestures toward
     the house, tells me

how his brother built it
     by hand, felling the timbers,

clearing the land, each pine
     craned into place

only a few feet from
     where it once stood,

enough trees left
     beside the road to pretend

the forest goes on
     unbroken for miles.

My uncle emerges
     victorious, unclenching

his right hand to reveal
     a shiny, red shotgun shell.

          §

The black bell of midnight
 is only a phone ringing

the world awake, the sound
 of trouble and my uncle's

voice saying *I told them,*
 saying *of course he really*

deserved it, I couldn't
 not do something this time,

just come, my quarter's up.
 My father is the pulse

of boot steps across linolcum,
 a truck door slammed.

From my bedroom window,
 I watch the glow

of two tail lights
 receding into one.

§

If the leaves creak
    inside casings of rust,

then my father is teaching me
    to chop wood.

How to stagger my feet,
    flex my knees,

the slight twist in the torso
    then the swing. How

to grip the handle
    just tight enough to feel

the wood slide through
    your right hand.

That's how it is, he says,
    though he says nothing.

A thousand measured strokes
    or one wild heave,

the rhythm of the axe,
    of a man pounding

all night on the door
    of his brother's house.

PASTORAL

Like middle schoolers grinding
behind the public restrooms
        these little birds chase
                each other endlessly
all scuffle and chirp

a minor cosmos
                within the larger
cosmos of falling leaves. Endlessly
I say
        but mean while I am

here, hearing it all: the oil-needy
        swings like some gripe
against childhood obesity,
        my drunk on the picnic table
snoring so strongly

you'd think he was
            tearing pages from
his high school yearbook. Still,

the slide shines, a landlocked lake.

Still, now, this used condom slung
        over
           one thin black branch,
orchid-white and lipped

with dew, serves proof that spring
        has come
again,
to refute the endless
           confetti of leaves.

MUSCLE MEMORY

How many linchpin unlabeled days suited up for my adulthood
and I swear still I'm standing
in that Saturday schoolyard counting slowly down
from three to one
then heaving the basketball over my shoulder,
miming the horn as the ball erases
the space between me
and my true future self, as the shot drops
in every twelfth time
and the crowd erupts from my throat, and there's nothing
left to want? How many hallelujahs
between the asshole and the saint?
Sometimes a minute passes, an hour,
and I find myself
marooned at the same south-facing window
staring at parked cars, unsure of why
my feet always lead me here
or what exactly I'm supposed to see.
Maybe that's all we are, two-dozen rote memories,
a meanness honed in pool halls, a cunning
in shopping malls, the last line of some cheesy poem
we were all made
to memorize in eighth grade. Tomorrow, I'll be an epiphany.
But for now let me be me
that summer I taught Ted, the aphasic fisherman,
to speak again, to type
three-line emails to his niece in Yakima
so he wouldn't be alone. He called me kid,
I remember, because he couldn't
remember my name, couldn't
remember the connector words—
"and" "is" "but"—
that tethered Portland to downpour.

So sweet, those almost haikus:
rose garden tuesday bloom turkey sandwich love hello soon.
Then one session he showed me
how to tie a fly—who knows what type—
looping the line
three quick times
around the body, binding filament and feather
with an deftness like breeze.
My buddy's wife cries to me that she wakes
each night to find him
assembling his rifle in his sleep like he's back in Tal Afar.
How long before that phantom urgency
lies down between them
and shuts its eyes?
Forget it.
Let us head to the bar.
Drink ourselves down to what we really are.
Sure, I'll probably pocket a pint glass,
get blasted and offer to drive.
Never mind it.
Drink up.
Get in.
This is only the hundredth of a thousand nights it takes
to make a perfect paper crane.

PAPER CRANES

This folding, unfolding, what is found where
a man turns inward on himself, turns

the corner to find his city somehow strange,
cornered by some change in himself, or the city,

the thousand cities each city is, as he walks
rehearsing the day, shrugging his coat

up around his shoulders, the paper
white, therefore, the city sudden with snow.

The next fold is introspection. The next, a river
running spit-creased through the city

from east to west, from here to wherever he just
was. So easy, the ornamental wings. How slender

the slender neck that holds the head. He folds
his arms against his chest against the cold

and continues on, toward a far white room
where he folds paper cranes for his son

as snow sifts all night outside their window,
the flakes so slow, hovering almost, some brief

species of flight, other men trudging through
other nights, the same cold, snow gathering on snow.

VINTAGE

These should be our lives: tandem bikes and rollerblades,
couples in coordinating outfits reclined at café tables
huffing tumblers of cabernet as if to savor even the musk
of the left-handed migrant who harvested the grapes
on an overcast day in a valley just east of Mendocino,
each ripe bunch lopped with a single flick of the wrist,
the same motion a woman now uses to brush away a fly
that obediently moves on toward people less reposed.
It's only a quarter past one, an hour I thought was still
reserved for poets and bums, but already the world seems
to be slipping into more comfortable clothes, open signs
turned over, women and men imitating cement mixers
in bed. I'd join them, but too much of my life has been
squandered listening to footfalls from the floor above.
How seldom are we essential! Whole existences spent
quality testing Lamborghinis or sporks, predicting futures
for imaginary commodities. Right now, I want to believe
that the toddler shoveling his overall pockets full of dirt
is really gathering soil samples to determine the ideal
conditions for propagating the doomsday seeds. Or this
woman crossing the street with her ten-gallon purse,
surely she's smuggling hand-carved Incan fertility gods
to save them from grave robbers or lonely archeologists.
But probably she's just heading home, the same as me,
after grabbing a smoothie and a few minutes of fresh air,
to reenter her rented life and watch sitcoms for a while.
She's already gone, disappeared to wherever strangers go,
the ecstasy of our life together lost, faded with the sirens
that scream toward another tragedy we'll never touch.
Maybe, at least, she'll water her half-dead house plants.
This evening, maybe, I'll jackhammer the keyboard keys

a bit harder. After, I'll sip my Franzia from a wine glass,
quaff all that ethanol and sweat, savoring the impossible
tartness that puckers the lips, invites you to kiss the floor
manager's forehead beneath the aurora of 10,000 watts,
to be with him, this once, in that hothouse in south Detroit.

2012

So the world is going to end again.
Everything undone
by fire or famine
or some theory about magnets,
the globe realigned
like a Rubik's cube.
After the plague,
there was land enough
for everyone, luxury crops
thrived, the soil rich with nitrogen
and death. Of course,
they didn't know
much about magnets.
The Mayans, it seems, knew
a bit of everything,
and so left
pictograms and shards of pottery
to allow us
our misinterpretations,
those wrong turns
that lead to new worlds.
I'm not talking about legacy.
The dead have no need
for trophies or truisms.
Not heaven, either.
All of us in God's green pocket
or not,
the suburbs suddenly for miles,
even the saints getting soft
in downtown eternity.
It's just if
I'm gone and you're gone
then what's lost? It seems sorrow is

always less than
absolute, always there is one
Noah, someone
chaste or lucky enough
to skirt catastrophe.
Let's say a woman, because
that would be nice,
and pregnant, because
the last hours are always spent
in lust or everlasting
embrace. She is underground,
thinking how strange it is
that the dead live
upstairs, as if
the old religion were true.
She wears a few seeds sewn into her coat,
because she likes the feel,
prayer beads between her fingers,
or so her body might feed
even in death.
But she won't die.
Instead, she waits until hunger
and wonder
are nearly one.
The earth is burnt or badly drawn.
It doesn't matter.
She plants the seeds
or stacks stone on stone.
She waits.
Later, she walks through
whatever has grown,
admiring the colors, the mineral
resolve, giving names
to those she doesn't know.

AS ONE STONE MAY BE USED TO SHAPE ANOTHER

Done making love, they walk along the Pacific,
he thinking how rehearsed
it all seems—the tidal flats polished
to high gloss, the bay
receding into sculpted outcroppings
of basalt, the hills mottled, rising
green to darker green to almost midnight
where the scrub pine and manzanita give way to Douglas fir
and then, farther, way up,
to fat black clouds
which massed inland an hour ago, leaving
even the scotch broom radiant and refreshed,
a few shafts of afternoon light across the water—like a commercial
for heaven or rehab.
Still, he carries a fine tiredness
inside his limbs, some semblance of sea-polished driftwood,
those minutes of passion
thrashed out of him and now her body
nooked beneath his arm.
They are walking because the March winds are brisk
or because they are an allegory
for love: a slow procession from one landmark
to the next, wonder
waning toward names,
a mild inertia which invites
the mind to dream.
She is thinking of an old boyfriend, a weekend
they spent, ten years ago, here. How strange
this stretch of sand still conjures him
so clearly, as if
the gulls which dervish overhead had been carving
those same infinities into the air
all this time. As if he meant anything to her now. Still,

scanning the rows of windows for their room,
some portion of her former self
lingering in the half-life of memory, a woman
half-dressed and less tired
giving herself over to the young man, that brief machine
between them, the one they made
working so hard at oblivion.
Did they even leave the room?
Did they get dressed and go down to the beach
and watch these funny little puffins sputtering
from rock to rock
staying, somehow, impossibly aloft?
That page of her memory is blank, whitened by time
or the maid who bleaches
each room clean, scrubs
the little islands of spent lust
off the duvet, the carpet, the curtains.
What persists is
that teenage urge rising
in her, the harbor of her husband's arm
around her shoulders, the idyllic
scene somehow congruent with those fantasies
a few moments ago.
"Let's go back," she says,
imagining how they'll make love again,
this time without decorum
or the regular progression from lip to thigh. And he,
a bit clarified by the salt air, thinks, yes,
twice in one afternoon, and then a heaping bowl of clam chowder.
And maybe that's enough.
Maybe there's no reason for her to envy the teenagers
pocketed between two dunes, the way

they chase their union, folding, unfolding,
trying to assume
the ocean's intermingledness.
It's enough, now, that he notices too, smiles.
It's enough to know their room is 103,
third window from the left.
So many windows staring always west.
And below, the bluff
rising from the beach, the ancient face—
they must have used stones—etched with love equations.

CACHE

Like a man rises to greet his life
at sunrise, the line of sky lifting into
light, and thinks of a woman
he had once, how she lifted for him
so slowly her skirt, and what came after.
Today he'll plummet into love
with every woman he meets, with a man
raising the gate of his bodega,
with eyelids even. Anything
that opens opens him. Until later.
Until lunch, maybe, when he's walking
past the steaming food carts longing
for perogies from this little Polish diner
that went under a few years ago,
potatoes and onions folded into dough,
so simple, so impossible to perfect,
and he wants suddenly only
perfection, to keep walking forever
or to fold himself beneath his bed sheets
and imitate oblivion. Like, above him,
these lazy doves decorating the trees,
each head tucked beneath a wing. Strange
to think such a white thing can carry
even a spoonful of darkness. But it must.

two

THE UNION OF GEOMETRY & ASH

In these distances between us, love, each inch
insinuates our avalanche,
each new weekday dawn marooned
at the kitchen window, a hangnail moon
loitering in the west, as a jay rips through
the frame, threads one last blue
into the morning's throat, into
the well-washed blue of your scrubs as you

whisper, *good morning.* An inch of milk
in each cup. Pinch of sugar. Brief ease for the ache
of black packed into bone all night, of days
delivered into years. The way
you lean and lift
on your right foot to kiss me, leave on your left.

Leave, on your left, whatever encumbers.
On your right, whatever wanes: the heart's archer, embers
cherried to ash, words.
What you keep I name *Whirlwind with Flightless Birds*.
What you are I cannot name, so this
flailing in the dark, blind flapping, a late iris
heisted from the neighbor's yard. Is everything
only barter for the beyond? An inkling

traced toward its extinction? If so,
then the mild Serengeti of our unmown lawn, two crows
scavenging a bag of chips, a spade
left out all fall and rusted the dozen shades
of the leaves that covered it. By what havoc
can we oust these antique feelings, this luxury of lack?

This luxury of lack: the live oak leafed with starlings
departing, black wings
and then black empty branches, winter
augmented. Our neighborhood schizophrenic never
seems lonely, only those of us
who haunt ourselves with less assertive ghosts,
swear some sudden other
must be balm for all our solitary hurts, a tether.

And still all day you thread
nectar-thick liquids and a few useful words
into the throats of broken children, chairs and tables
hammered solid with a pocketful
of consonants. I am the stutter
you must sing smooth. You are the darkness that proves stars.

You are the darkness that proves stars once were
these empty lawn chairs facing east, flowers
weeks dead but still fragrant,
a woman across the street troweling the earth, bent
toward whatever penance drives
each green thing up, whatever give
in the good meat gives finally out to grace.
How many have failed at our life? For this,

the bangers bump Chicano rap and the sun
loves each thing equally. Sometimes a red balloon
coasting over rooftops seeks no surrogate
inside your chest and simply drifts out
over the city ever downward.
Sometimes one hawk, circling, is enough to wind the world.

Enough to wind the world, to stoke the broken engines
of thought that peter out among
the head lettuce gone to seed. And still I have no name
for the way your hands tame
some leisure into my least nerve, for six dandelions
in a sawed-off coke can,
a telephone pole bookended by oaks.
Next lesson: the concentration of rocks.

But substitute illusions will not do. No more
than visualizing figures
in a constellation of pocket change, the theory of an umbrella
against rain. The will
is not well-wrought enough to haggle starlight
from a TV screen. A bird is more than flight.

A bird is more than flight for any branch that bends
against arrival. The ash end
of his cigarette seeps brief branches of smoke
but the man in his bathrobe, just awake
at noon, isn't worried for the birds
but trying, with one foot, to unkink the garden hose
so he can water the half-dead mums
his girlfriend planted to make the place more homey.

And you, at work, are eating fruit salad or jotting down notes
on the best way to elicit
sounds from a mouth made of holes,
charting in your mind each nerve, its role,
the branch it travels back to the spine
as your mind back to me a moment, then back again.

A moment, then, back again the hummingbird
plunges, confusing one red shard
of flower pot for the salvia it once contained.
So should be our sins: to spend
ourselves out too perfectly and often,
to passion some rationale from the broken
paving stones that lead toward
evening, the crippled crab apple in the side yard.

Let me be the savant of your slightest
vacancy, one shoelace in a makeshift nest,
a vein of quartz rivered through
more common rock, the immigrant work crew
fashioning, groove for groove,
a brand new house where someone else will live.

Someone else will live with these
questions like a sleepy cat circling their feet. But we
prefer dogs, to be hound-bound and driven
into the loose last logic of tin
roofs rusted the color of earth, a parakeet
this far north, fruit so sweet
just one more day would see it ruined. But
tablecloths and backhoes and light.

But remember that night just after we met?
The moon snooping through the window wet
with rain, through the fogged-up glass,
looked like a cop's flashlight, then was.
We were only talking, my hands in my pockets.
And still it felt like we'd been found out.

Like we'd been found, out wandering the deserts
west of here, what asserts
itself as savior is sometimes just more sand.
Other times, the far-off sound
of the interstate is ocean enough to soothe.
And in between are weeds, tires worn smooth
with use, the heft of half-lit days
laced with a casual loss that coins us, stays.

To do: recalibrate the compass east, learn
the shorthand of three-hundred acres burned
by wildfire and the flowers that flourish
afterward, pray to the god of silverfish
and boot heels, betray
my mindset, mend the back fence but not quite all the way.

But not quite all the way, no closer
than a kiddy pool brimming with rainwater
approaches the Pacific, its depth and hue,
can I come to knowing you.
I marvel too much the improvised garden
of your underwear drying on the backs of chairs, cotton
intuiting your contours
the way a scrub jay, improvising, reveals the air.

Once, this would have been enough:
to propagate unhaunted places, claim proof
in the lengthening evening shadows
that we are exiled mostly within ourselves. Even now,
these words seem understudy
to intimations less vagrant: cut grass, sirens, your body.

Cut grass sirens your body the way crickets ratchet
moonlight into each
sleeping thing. I can't explain.
All these rote revivals just sparkle and wane.
But when, as we too seldom do, the fence rails
resume their former life as pines, cull
the forest from one warped board,
the late light lingers, clear, undivided,

and we harbor each other briefly home.
It's not enough, I know. So quickly we dim
and continue on, map
the world by monuments only. What little there is to keep
we must keep close: love notes
yellowing in drawers, butterflies pinned beneath glass.

Butterflies pinned beneath glass. Young junkie,
in a little girl's pink unicorn backpack,
hounding the corner bus stop for half-spent
cigarettes. Cement
cracking where roots run through. Two clocks
three minutes apart. We speak
most fluently in finger tips and tongues,
rough seductions from the heart's velvet lounge.

But flesh is too physical to last. I want
demarcations more darkly inked, a storefront
to display our insecurities. I want you
always, as now, singing as you speed through
the backstreets home, the scenery
all inertia and blur, the whine of brakes in the driveway.

The whine of brakes in the driveway is an instrument
best played in pairs: you bent
to gather what the day requires
each of us to carry home, me holding the door
and the dogs back. Again we flare,
then atrophy into our former selves. Two beers,
the day doled out in incidents, fruit
falling in the yard as the shoes off your feet.

I can't say what is lost in all this relapse.
Each city, giant and shining, built on the collapse
of another just as bright. But tonight,
I watch a few fireflies reiterate
the whole history of passion,
flashing like beacons from the far edge of the ocean.

From the far edge of the ocean, you drift
into our room. Even these dreams are too swift
to outfit with flesh, to populate
past our furthest doubt. Anyway, it's late.
What you mumble in your sleep I'll take
for song, lyrics to the sand-sifted music
of passing cars, password
for those dim anterooms in which we usually reside.

If our lives are nearly forfeit,
tamed by shopping lists and time, don't forget
even these half-hushed passions, the thinnest whisper,
must have left our lips as fervor,
as something mostly holy and built for flight, to persist
in these distances between us.

three

PRODIGAL

From the rebuilt Buick a few spare parts,
from the earth's precession a backdoor
for havoc to hurry through. From me to you
a thousand miles and my condolences
about a thousand things. You pick.
Say global warming, I'll clear some space
in the fridge for you. Say your shattered
heart, I'll buy a thousand shares
of duct tape. Nothing? Still, here, I sit,
watching the sun rise with more flair
than necessary, counting the dead
houseflies that punctuate the white sill,
even their corpses decked out
in iridescence and me always feeling
a bit unprepared, wishing I could hear
myself when I holler, *here I am*! But
it's too early for hollering. Might as well
enumerate each absence and label it
a song. Here is a coast; here, a harbor.
From here to there. In the hearsay
of the great hereafter. Here goes nothing.

GATHERING THE RAIN

Maybe it's the light this time of year, the wayward gray
half-spent light, that calls each thing

out of itself, insists the slightest entity
harbor both shadow and form,

leaving you to marvel a moment
the green, green of elms so green
that any other season seems instantly a lie,

a dream, which it is,

but no more so than this, this infant autumn
or the brief seasons between each drop of rain,

the first fat drop, a tap on the shoulder,
and if you turned

you would see

yourself, sixteen, scuffing the other way down Division
toward a vacant filled with vacancies—

the migrant affections of half-drunk schoolgirls,
the self-surgery in sweating rooms,
two boys practicing their manhood

in the alley, pounding each other
as the crowd pushes close and cheers, satisfied

no matter who wins, who is lost
forever to that scuffle each of us plays out

inside ourselves—but you can't follow him,
because that vacant is a pet store now,

and the cheering of the crowd
is only this whisper of lightly falling rain, each memory

stitched so loosely into the last,
threaded through by rain, by loss itself,

the luster of the trees already growing tame.

§

If what is lost is more than what is carried,
are you a thimbleful

of water offered to the ocean? A drop of rain
touching its borders only as it falls?

Are you still staring at a tree
as cars cascade past, as the old homes are torn down

and built up and torn down again

in the time it takes
you to turn back toward yourself and
button your coat? Oh, right,

you never turned. But why then this feral feeling
rising with steam off the concrete?

Why this urge to wear your eyes
like the boarded windows of a vacant? To see

nothing and so be
blind at least by choice? To carry him

the two miles home
only to hang him up by the door with your wet coat?

If what is lost is really only lost?

§

Then maybe it was your father's life that found you
staring down some other trees

from the far end of a park bench, chirping
for birds that had already flown

or knew you had nothing to offer
but pocket lint and words. So easily you could have slipped

away, settled into the passenger's seat
of that primer-gray Cutlass idling

in the parking lot, those black windows reflecting
the anticipation of junkies and kids

like you. So easily you slipped away,

into your father's dreams, where bright birds pecked
the corners of the day

until each day was small enough to fit
into his breast pocket, to be carried, piecemeal

as the rain that found him
heading west from West Virginia

until the Pacific rose up and whispered, *no farther.*
Your father, almost your age then, when

he stepped down from the running board
of that battered blue Toyota pickup
onto the ash-soft earth of Oregon, stepped

into your mother's hands, hands
like two small white bowls

to hold the rain, to hold a son

or the shape of his leaving, driving east
as the rain tapers to almost nothing,

as a blue pickup passes going the other way
with your father—you nod—behind the wheel.

§

There was a girl, because there's always a girl.
She said, *no farther.*

As if on cue, the rain spilled over, and you
offered her your coat. She scuffed the other way

down Division. She left you stranded
like a tree. She was the dry circle beneath a tree,

a place the rain never touched.

You saw her in the back seat of each passing car.

Sometimes you're not sure
you've ever seen her, only

a jostling in the leaves way up where
the rain begins. But that was years ago.

You are bone-soaked, now.

You are scattered

as the rain. You are

walking the two miles home to her,
to climb into that vacancy in her, which is

the shape of your mother's hands,
your father's hunger, is everything you can take,

besides pocket lint and whispers,
the light this time of year,

these dreams that catch the world awake.

§

The rain unravels and moves east, easing up, lasting
longer than a thing this slight should,

so light and constant it might not even be
rain anymore, only the white noise

an infant falls asleep to each night, the last
scatter of seed spilling from an old man's hand

where he sits on the far end of a park bench,
the pigeons massing at his feet,

a few drops, a few more seeds,
a slight palsy in his outstretched hand
that seems matched by the motion of the birds

bobbing to fetch the seed, the gray-white cloud
of birds so dense they resemble a tiny sky,
a storm of birds maybe making a tiny rain.

But the rain has stopped. And the pigeons,
all at once, scatter and drift east, all

except the last, brave or too badly maimed,
pecking aimlessly the black earth,

its wings rising and falling and rising, the feathers
white against gray and darker gray, ash

against almost black, the faint storm
of greens and purples, glazed, as if with rain,
the tremor in the wings settling a little

as it finds his fingers, as it climbs into the empty hand.

BRIEF MEMORY CARRYING A TWIG IN ITS BEAK

All those fires
my father

kindled with
yesterday's news

as I watched
the pages blacken

and flap, then
rise as crows.

LETTER TO H.

Strange to write for you, to you, this. You, who I knew nearly a year,
that nervous first year of college, when, from separate worlds, we
entered another together. It was chance. Our names paired
on some list we never had any say in, your loud bad music, my . . .
(see how quickly I start talking about myself). Of course you see
nothing now: your eyes collapsed to flower pots, your baby fat finally
gone. You, who never drank because your father, then you were dead.
I thought about you yesterday, though I hadn't in months, years.
An old blue pickup, like yours, with a chubby kid thumbing the wheel.
Where was he going in such a hurry? Where are you?
In all your innocence, eighteen, the answer seems easy—if you believe
in all that. You did. Mostly I hope you're right. That summer
the phone said you were thrown from the truck, an awkward flight,
a rock, the phone said. They put you in the ground the next week.
I transferred that fall. I probably never would've seen you again.
Thought of you less. Dirty clothes shoved beneath your bed,
teenage fantasies commingling in your mind. You would've been
a good man, not so ambitious as to do much harm, kind.
I wish this letter were longer, but already the words feel like slander.
I hope they played speed metal at your funeral, buried you
in your busted, black high tops. You lived so far away. Farther now.

TREES OR MEMORIES

How even night breeds light
  with time, the eye's dim

wattage dialed up, pitch black
  sapped back to almost day.

Say a name, any name
  enough, and watch that face

recede toward formlessness.
  And so to call out too often

is to call to nothing,
  anything: a silver dollar

slipped inside a pocket, the lit
  candle rehearsing its one

thought, a dead man's arms
  folded neatly as a love note.

It's for you. It reads: the dead
  dead long enough live

again. Trees or memories.
  One life leavened, folded into

the next. Feather tucked
  into feather, so that the air

might be held a moment again.
  Up or in. A breath folded across

the tongue, sung or softly
   spoken, a name, a note. It says:

A dark road goes on forever.
   It says: If you are reading this

there must be light enough.

WINTER COAT

Happiness, you are the bright red lining
of the dark winter coat
Grief wears inside out.
                    —Charles Simic

My happiness has three buttons:
silver, golden, self-destruct.
My happiness is fleece-lined
and out of style, like the coat
my mother made me in fifth grade,
the coat I slipped free from
each morning just before
the Elementary came into view.
A few leaves flagging from the branches,
her hands frantically waving
from the window. Yes, grief.
But sometimes as simple as slipping
on a coat and wandering out
into the wide world, where
the bus stop strangers huddle
close as lovers and the wind
tunes every hollow toward a song.
Let's hum along. Let's walk
arm in arm, so close there's no need
for coats, no need to acknowledge
the man on the corner who
makes a home of his old coat
or to think of the woman right now
dying in a country far away.
Let someone else lay a coat
across her face. This poem
is the one where two lovers
spread their coats out in a field

in winter to make a bed then
a little love, to have a picnic
of wax-covered cheese and baguettes
and bicker over the names of birds
and meander back through town
admiring the little ghosts
their words make, the little ghosts
their lives wake, the strangers
at every window watching them
pass like a day. And there she is,
in the window of our house,
my mother. It's cold out there,
she is saying. Don't forget your coat.

THEORY OF MIND

Not so difficult now to imagine his mind unable to imagine mine,
to wonder at another's actions and find them
mostly baffling. In my memory,
which seems itself
made up of many minds, I enter
that cramped basement classroom
with its two other specialists and fifteen three-year-olds,
and find him, Noah, standing
in front of the window fan, his bowl cut fluttering
in the wind, just standing
there, transfixed,
with his red backpack and his autism.
Those crusty-eyed mornings and drooly afternoons,
those impossibly long first days of adulthood
I spent doling out
language and stale animal crackers,
offering each child the words but never quite
knowing how to name the vacancy inside me
when my coaxing failed, when silence spilled over
like water in the sink. There was no malice in it,
no conspiracy. It was nothing
like those nights with the girl I was with then, those mute hours
our apartment seemed constructed
of constantly shifting walls. That's it,
it was nothing
like anything I knew then, the world
revised by a single consciousness
not my own, the tethers between
two people suddenly cut.
I had a theory that autism might just be
the next detour in our evolution,
that cell phones and the mercury-teeming seas
would tincture us toward

a million micro-worlds.
I was probably reading Descartes,
surviving another six months of drizzle
and the education that some disabilities are not so easily seen.

Am I just talking to myself again?
I feel it sometimes so much, the honing
sense of singularity,
that to brush past a stranger on the sidewalk is to break
free of my skin, that even
the daily curses of our neighborhood schizophrenic, a man
who calls me Charlie
and warns me always that Mother is waiting,
crazy with grief,
even his half-lit fantasy is flesh enough
to conjure a momentary corner we share like cheap wine.
It's a dream.
My mother lives two thousand miles from here.
It's Kristin who waits three blocks away
in our rented life
for the dollar tacos I tote home
and a kiss on the cheek. It's my angel
who waits for that instant when
whatever hunger delivers us here
to there, whatever spasm of space, is squandered in the sudden
confetti of late leaves, country music
from a window I never find.
It's a dream.
The red backpack was empty.
No inviolate city shimmered inside
the mechanized breeze of the box fan.
By spring, he'd mastered the classroom routines,
a few phrases.

Still, most mornings I'd find him
standing there, rocking
almost imperceptibly from foot to foot,
unflinching when I tapped him twice on the right shoulder
and said, "Good morning, Noah."
Was the sand table really full of sinking ships?
Is each word we speak a tiny death?
A few times—for what reason?—he turned to me,
vacant as if scanning some great distance,
a distance greater than the years
from now to then,
from here to where I wait
and the other maimed darlings all wobble through their orbits
or mouth the plastic fruit,
and he, found, finds the words and, finally, me.
"Good morning, Noah," he says.

STUTTER

Say trees. Say these sycamores frenzied
   in wind. Again. No matter if the leaves

turn, tongue-tied and tremoring, no
   matter if you burn back to that first

urge to green. Say burl. Say wooden
   is the tongue too tautly strung, the words

all sputter and sheen—this makeshift
   of branch-shadows, the mouth-cave

undone by breeze. Relax the axeman
   in your throat. If not, please, at least

recite one thing you know by heart:
   your telephone number, a prayer

from Sunday school. If logic leaves you
   lock-jawed still, and the trees tatter

toward birds, just stand there quaking,
   root-shaken and shuttered. Say world.

GHOST TOWNS OF THE OLD WEST

His fingers trace the façade, in a book,
of some deceased saloon, the noon sun
illuminating forever the dust and a dozen men
who loiter beneath a rough-cut sign,
like signs themselves for towns returned
to dust. Once, he could have read the captions,
would have cornered you and told you how
it was water made the west, not gold,
but his eyes are bad now and his memory
not much better, the stories a patchwork
of Navajo blankets and his granddaughter's
golden hair. Or how The Kid cheated
Death and Pat Garret, rode north to Detroit
where he turned precision parts forty years
for Chrysler, bet the dogs, went by Willy.
If you ask, he'll let you look, grin
as you read the names—Canyon Diablo,
Sumner, Carson City—as if each were
password to some secret life: a woman,
his wife, calling to him from a rented room
above the bar, tempting him to slip through
the caballeros and the years, to ascend
the beer-soaked staircase as if climbing free
of his own body, and ease back the door
and enter, and be mingled with her forever.
But it's only a fantasy, a figment thin as paper,
and she, the dust that gilds the edge
of dog-eared pages. So there is nothing to do
but listen as he tells you about a cache
of silver coins buried in the black hills,
a palomino hurling herself toward death
two-hundred miles to save her gut-shot rider;

there is nothing to say when he begins
whispering his wife's name then goes silent,
as if he's forgotten you're there. Maybe he has.
Maybe you're gone. And there is no one
to watch him touch each photo like a wrist:
the luster of an army Colt, a woman holding
the hem of her dress a few inches above the dust.

LOUISE, 63, TRIES TO SAY UMBRELLA

though carousel comes out,
something about circles
or those first fat drops
of rain deliberate
as fingertips touching
the Wurlitzer to life. Or
maybe it's the barker's voice,
so strut-strung and lifted,
wide enough to invite
the whole night into
his throat, his high-arched
palate bright pink, pink
as a little girl's umbrella.
Or is it the night itself,
opening, so many strangers
pushing past her that
to stop and stare up into
the darkness is to stand
at the still center of a sudden
storm. You can't touch
her. And so you wander
from booth to booth,
pretending the games
aren't rigged, side-saddling
the fluorescent appaloosa
named Happenstance,
until the gates are locked
and the carnival torn down
and moved, or you are
moved then torn down

then moved again, to where
she stands in her robe
in the harsh light in the lobby
of the outpatient hospital,
calling you by the name
her dead husband once wore,
you, who lead her toward
the window and try to
accompany each stray word
safely home. Don't worry.
If it's raining when you go,
you can borrow her carousel.

SKETCH WITH YELLOW ASTERISK

for Tommy

What first strikes you is the scale, the man—we know he's a man
because she's drawn a black hat—
looming tall as the house beside him, the woman
in her triangle skirt to his left,
half his height, and stationed slightly closer
to the girl, a self-portrait
with *a polka dot rectangle dress and spaghetti hair.*
In reality, this girl beside me,
with her consolation of crayons,
has hair more russet, less curly, a nest
of tangles I've never noticed. (In reality, this was years ago,
the last time I saw her, though
I still keep the picture in my bottom desk drawer.)
Her figures all float a half-inch above
the grass, grass grown as long as the girl's legs,
obscuring the threshold
of the door that leads, I would guess, to this very couch,
this room littered with toys, coverless books, therapy equipment.
I'm waiting for her mother, in the other room,
to sign the papers so I can close the file.
The girl hums beside me,
adding a second green to the grass, two windows
though this house has only one,
a few birds just so we know
the sky is there. Outside, the sky is almost paper-white,
but more intricate, so many gradations
from cotton to milk to baby powder
to that bluish white they paint dead people on TV.
A man is walking his dog, a dachshund, like comic relief
too early in the scene, and I want to follow them
home or out into the streets of Portland
where people are eating pastries or waiting for the bus

or singing badly a pop song while they drive. I want
to ignore the box of donated clothes his mother handed me,
each item folded with care
like a memory, to leave this room behind,
one-dimensional as the picture the girl
tells me is finished. There are flowers now
because, in childhood, it is always or almost
spring. She's added a chimney with smoke, I'll say
to symbolize the fire at the heart of things.
And in the background, atop a small, floating hill, more
chimneys or upright cigarettes,
the same smoke snaking skyward in the same smoke-gray shade,
and one tiny star, an asterisk in canary yellow
off to the side. I'll ask her now, for you,
what it's supposed to be, though I remember clearly
that yellow sweatshirt he always wore,
and how she told me, *that's Tommy.*
Mom says he's with grandma and grandpa now.
And when I hesitated, still unsure of what she'd drawn,
she added, *they live in Pittsburgh.*
And so I'm writing this
because I found the picture yesterday while hunting for thumb tacks
and remembered him
growing thin, and thinner, and now so thin
he can live inside this picture his sister drew.
And now I can almost convince myself
she's right: the dead living together in some city
tough enough to make them feel alive again,
pulling double shifts down at the plant
because eternity can get tedious,
smoke blooming from the stacks
because how else could heaven rest on a girder of cloud.
And we, the living, go on

pulling shifts or making love or writing poems and then, done,
stroll the neighborhood
looking for ourselves and those recesses
where the dead shiver birches or kindle the throats
of small birds, and sometimes
the scale seems funny, and dusk is a window
flung suddenly open. And you just stand there,
hearing the wind, a sound like someone sweeping up in all that
grass gone long.

REFRAIN

It's so simple: the chair one day empty
and the next
a new old lady spooning soup.

Of course the Chinese cherry flourished when dressed
with windfall

but pruning I still can't understand,

Purgation and Holiness strolling hand in hand,
thinking how the other's inner thigh might feel
but knowing that not knowing

aches as good as anything. A clarity,

I suppose. High windows overlooking the city.
You think, *the river's sweet amnesia . . .*

then think of the ward women forgetting
themselves, growing simple but not

the simple you seek riding your bike to work,
reading the dictionary,
planting radishes you could buy for a buck a bunch.

Not the garden, but hours of earth.
Not the view, but what opens in you.

As a man walks beside the river so as to slip slowly away
from himself, easy in the inertia of other things.
The birds, dispersing. Thoughts.

The heart, a fist of thistles.

The heart, an empty chair.

FOR OUR CHILD-TO-BE

Son, daughter, green dinosaur your mother some nights dreams
you are, what can I say?
I've spent three nights trying to write this line
and now it's done. I guess
that's how it is. You wager a week, a year,
half your life waiting
to brush up against whatever ache
drove our ancestors to name the stars, and then you
notice constellations
blooming in a scatter of roadside daffodils.
It's best just to laugh.
Pick a few, give them away.

Tonight, though, I watch the moon proceed across the sky,
one white bead on God's black abacus,
and wish I could tell you
this world is a just and gentle place.
I'll save that lie for tomorrow, fold it twice
and let it winter in a shoebox
with all those mementos you won't believe: my love
letters, yellowed Polaroids, visions
tinged with the light of galaxies
long collapsed into iron. All I can say is
your mother owns a tree limb's gift for birds.
My gray moods have nothing to do with you.
And sometimes, late summer,
when the swifts careen from the eaves
or someone brushes, gently, the hair out of your eyes,
as if to erase that blindness we choose
to bear and believe, the world pauses, almost,
and we lapse into grace.

NOTES

The epigraph is taken from Martin Heidegger's essay "Who is Nietzsche's Zarathustra?"

The line "Here is a coast; here is a harbor" is from Elizabeth Bishop's poem "Arrival at Santos."

"Muscle Memory" is for Andrew Dutton.

ACKNOWLEDGMENTS

Many thanks to the editors of the following publications where poems in this collection first appeared:

Borderlands: Sonnet 4 from "The Union of Geometry & Ash"

Cellpoems: "Brief Memory Carrying a Twig in Its Beak"

Hayden's Ferry Review: "The Book of Love" and "For Our Child-To-Be"

Iron Horse Literary Review: "Take This Waltz"

Missouri Review: "As One Stone May be Used to Shape Another," "Finches," "Sketch with Yellow Asterisk," and "Strange Shapes the Night Makes"

Raleigh Review: "Cache"

THRUSH: "Prodigal"

I am grateful to The Michener Center for Writers, the E. L. Keene Prize, and The Dorothy Sargent Rosenberg Memorial Fund for support essential to the completion of this project.

I am indebted to all those who helped shape this book, including Michael Adams, David Wevill, Dean Young, Harvey Hix, Mary Ruefle, David Biespiel, Rebecca Starks, Andrew Dutton, Zeb Taylor, Patrick Ryan Frank, Laura Dixon, Carolina Ebeid, Shamala Gallagher, Kevin Powers, Nicole Cullen, and Ryan Cannon for "Spoon."

Thanks to my parents, who kept giving me books even when I said reading was boring.

To Kristin and Porter, always.

ABOUT THE AUTHOR

Josh Booton was born and raised in Portland, Oregon. He is a graduate of the Michener Center for Writers at The University of Texas at Austin, where he was awarded the 2011 Keene Prize in Literature. He works as a speech therapist in an outpatient rehab hospital.